BOON

fifty poems

Karl Elder

ISBN: 978-93-6354-877-0

First Edition: 2025
Rs. 200/-

Cyberwit.net
HIG 45 Kaushambi Kunj, Kalindipuram
Allahabad - 211011 (U.P.) India
http://www.cyberwit.net
Tel: +(91) 9415091004
E-mail: info@cyberwit.net

Printed at Repro India Limited.

Acknowledgments:

Thanks to editors of the following publications in which some of the work of *Boon* first appeared, albeit in somewhat, slightly revised form with respect to a couple of pieces.

Journals:

Bramble

Last Stanza Poetry Journal

Literature Today

The Muse: An International Journal of Poetry

Nimrod International Journal of Prose and Poetry

Peninsula Pulse

Poetry Hall

Reed Magazine

Verse Wisconsin

Wisconsin Fellowship of Poets Museletter

Wisconsin Poets' Calendar

Anthologies:

Harmonic Verse

Intersections: Art and Poetry

Minute Musings: Short and Contemplative Poems

Walt Whitman Bicentennial Poems

Walt Whitman 205

When It Rains It Pours

Cover illustration:

iStock

credit: jorgeantonio

Contents

The Mansion

Dear Reader,

Though you are not here,
suddenly you are,
this missive practically
missing.

It's quite a start—
you in my face
and the usual trace
of wonder in the voice,
that third party,
that Tinkerbelle from hell,
the little tart,
who sits on my shoulder, leans toward,
and whispers in your ear
words I strain to hear.

Dear Poet,

Thanks for the card, the note.
We're at a loss for words
at your offer to host us.
The island is lovely.
We vacationed there once,
enquired, even, about a timeshare,
but your indigenous variety
of mosquito sends us elsewhere,
its tiny engine's whine
out of nowhere,
its itty-bitty
bite.

Forgive our irritation, the itch,
but we bought a plot,
a lot by our neighborhood church,
instead. Forgive also
the brevity of this
in the face of your long-standing invitation,
but we want to get
it in the mail before we forget.

The Recapitulation

Until a man spends time
alone with his heart
he cannot know who he is.

Such is the wisdom of one
who mothers a goldfish
abandoned by his children.

Slowly he remembers what's
always been on his mind
like echoes empty of sound

in synch now with the gills
as if his ears have eyes
just as the fish has eyes of

the embryo the man once was—
startled from the start—
as if for a time he forgot

what is meant, with a heart
like this, to be human—
half of man, half of woman.

The Mansion

We turn onto an old access newly paved
and nearly hidden. For a reason
I cannot fathom I'm glad there are

these paths that wind through pastures
abundant with sun, revealing one by one
new houses the size of suburban churches.

So what if we know we don't belong.
But for a twelve-year-old son scolding
us over my shoulder for slowing down

before the expanse of a particular lawn,
we'd not be here in the first place.
Ever since he was young he's talked

about mansions. He wants to own one.
I guess we're here to egg him on. "How
do you live in twenty-one rooms at once?"

is a dumb question I almost ask him.
Luckily I've got the savvy to save it,
count, instead, three chimneys on one

roof. There are two houses we can see
right through—so huge the windows above
the entryways, so wide the light inside.

I wonder out loud about privacy, does
he think the owners think they have any.
I don't tell him it's all part of his

education, this little excursion on our
way back from the mall. An hour later
we turn into our subdivision. A couple

of blocks and our own property appears,
a two-story, gray and red, dwarfed from
the back by ash, birch, cedar, and oak—

the tallest trees in town. It's a miracle
whatever lord allows us to live here,
like the rented houses we were raised in,

only new—brand new. My wife and I know
this is *our* mansion, maybe our last home.
Coming to a stop, I say to him I never want

to pack another box; just bury me in back.
I tell him this, too, is his lot: he's already rich.
Engine off, we hear a soft, but haughty "*humph.*"

727

So few pass over here so low
it was like a tornado roared over,
tore the fog a hole
so we nearly read the rivets.

O winged sardines
granting me eyes again
vacations we drive by O'Hare
seeing you land or bank out of there
maybe a half mile off
yet so large
and thus close,
as if a replica of yourself,
as if a toy impossible to hold.

Suppose I'll always marvel at the magic,
stepping off in Atlanta once, thinking
how exact this illusion, how precisely
detailed these people here to greet us,
just like in the picture of them back home.

From the look on their faces
they can't believe we're here.
Well, probably we are
just as one day in the future
we'll be standing there, *here*
in the wake of its thrust,
wondering where in the world
could it be coming from
as if, in turn, it had nowhere to land
but our groundless fear.

Anecdote of the Bottle

Like a rogue lunar vehicle
This disposable water bottle
With a nose that seemingly
Knows its noise annoys

Rolls on the gravel roof
Outside the window of Room 564
Of the Hilton in the City of Wind
Breathing out and in

So the bottle in its fits of stops
And starts reverses, darts, parks—
Unmolested weathervane—
Then rotates as if a needle

On a compass that itself
Is searching for direction
Which can only be had
Like nothing else in Illinois.

Where a Hawk Caught a Dove

Lickity-split—heard,
sensed a hawk hit
the feeder window, thud

in an eruption of wings,
or call it dud,
note a bass drum sings,

why the surprise,
next day, outside,
before our eyes:

like a pupil, but red,
and flawed iris spread,
that soft, gray feather bed—

the way of the world
said, unfurled,
looking back at you.

March

The shape a snowbank takes
the rain makes
out the corner of your eye
driving by—
a tanish tinge
like the wet fringe
of a polar bear
slumbering on her
side, suddenly sprung
up among
us to lumber
across an asphalt tundra—thunder.

Of Lions and Lambs

It’s not enough of a Sunday to say
divine sounds abound in their counterweight, quiet,
as wind through cord on the bare flagpole hums
and strums like a harp, that river willow
beyond the diamond down the hill,
while the overlay of voices, the chopped
consonants, the sporadic vowels, is absent,
while a cop’s the only car in the parking lot,
while it, too, seems abandoned, because the season
has begun, because any moment Monday,
outside or in, along with shouts
shots may ring out.

Finding My Butt with Both Hands

In one life you're out in left field
and in the next your boy is at the batter's box
and you're the manager, rather,
a coach in this town.

It's two outs, bottom of the ninth,
tied, with nobody on.
The season, too, is winding down.
You've yet to win one.

You have, with help of texts,
taught them the game.
Hands tucked in your back pockets,
you kick the dust off third base and pace.

You've talked a lot about having fun,
how winning's less important than heart.
You stop, look toward the plate. Without a sound
your stance is the sign for home run.

The Dinner Party

An evening of exercising the ear, then a walk east
on Emerson, the very street where—no lie—
I was conceived and somehow now have returned,
I'm at a dinner party, late, where I lean lightly to my left
and point with my spoon to Albert Goldbarth's bowl
of John and Sue's, our host and hostess's, pumpkin soup,
declaring around a mouthful, "Ummm, it's like baby food for adults,"
and Albert, never one to leave undone a tune or routine,
unleashes with a tongue languid as mine from lapping red
the last half hour from great stoneware goblets a line about black
velvet,
which makes such sense, tactilely, I need not understand it
and reaching across my right arm still holding the spoon
to cradle the goblet in my left hand, I see for the first time since
being seated
the centerpiece, an object the size of a pumpkin,
which becomes a pumpkin, a real live pumpkin not two feet from
my face,
and I want, presently, my high chair, want Sue and John
to send everyone to the living room for their coffee and pumpkin
cheesecake,
except I want to keep Albert here, my talking bear, and I want John
to take away the goblet and Sue to hold my spoon in her elegant
mother's hand
and play airplane and hangar with my mouth until, their little pumpkin,
I fall asleep, and in big John's big arms as he ascends the stairs
I will for an instant catch sight of something out the window at
the landing,

something bald, something orange set on the stage before the
black curtain
so old it has holes in it, pinpoints of light, white,
and over John's shoulder and behind him I shall point
before I fall back asleep, and before I'm done pointing,
just as John mounts the second flight, he shall have heard me
mumble,
"boon."

O Moon

O moon,
In stark and dark November, why
When I've turned out the last light,
This thought
I might remain
To stare all night
In the manner I now regard moonlight,
Soft and ubiquitous
Throughout the house,
As though the timbers
Are akin to the trees outside,
Themselves mere skeletons of themselves
Cast in ghost light,
Moonlight,
Shadow of sunlight,
O moon,
Whom I abandoned for poems.

Apparitions

I Know Your Face

but the name is a bubble in glass
into which I peer,

nearly hear it whispered,
drawn in the sand of an island

yet unrisen under ocean
on a planet of a phantom system

where waves, large shards,
swell, sway, dissipate

as if liquid slate the instant
I stretch for any instrument,

the would-be script
destined to a denizen

of incalculable recollections,
flashes sans synapses,

the gray velvet vistas,
dawn donning itself and fading

pointillism of stars or thinnest
spun filament of tungsten

in a lightbulb, shaken—
softest tinkle shorn of its *t*

like a dead daddy longlegs
caught in a hoary old bottle.

The Face of the Buddha

Now here's a curious cow,
handsomely numb
among rear ends all in a row,
frozen to the dawn like

the lifeblood just got
sucked out all of them.
And who better to prove
that the blood is but milk

if not this bolder (older?)
sister of the herd, turned
opposite the sun toward
the I of the beholder,

the jogger slowing down,
as the two study one another
as if beyond the beyond
with a look they look upon.

Flame

a medley

What makes a moth of the eye.
Rose in a match head, un-bloomed.
Blind spot in the side of night.

What's wholly unholy in the hole.
Satan unwrapping his gift of smoke.
Tethered pennant in an updraft.

Black plague on prairie grass, endemic.
Smarting from lightning's crooked needle.
Piranhas stripping branches to the bone.

Mirror trained on the devil's eyes.
Yellow going red going orange gone gold.
Fringe running along a log.

In and out of repose, the fancydancer's ghost.
Anti-matter, anti-gravity, science friction.

11/11

Wind knocked the wind
out of itself
and took itself with it.

Ablaze now at sunrise,
a small maple uphill
has long hung on,
all crimson on a stick.

It's a day so crisp, as
still as an old stump,
the mole knows crows
by their ebony throats,

while only yesterday
a momentary man
made of leaves rose—
a slow, then swift whir—

so gauche a ghost gone
so adroit its
art turned deaf the ear.

Vista on a Winter Eve's Walk

Clone after clone
of a jilted bride

storming off,
gowns trailing,

turning ribbons
running uphill

or below light poles
a horizontal waterfall

in amber waves
of albino grain,

mares' tails among—
throngs—then become

a shrunken herd
of drunken dust devils

funneled to a tunnel
of opaque dark but

not before a sleeping
sheepdog, all awash,

bolts up, chasing
its tail, and, as if

with the quick
lash of a whip,

quits.

Strange Fruit

Hat's off to you, rutabaga, whom
I couldn't spell to look you up
to find in what vines you dwell,
over whose bins you may
hang, plumb, plump, as now,
without knowledge,
I picture you plump.

Now, rutabaga, it's a mystery
why I mouth your name,
thrusting hand and with it my head,
bowing for the balled, wayward sock
at the back of the dryer's drum
inert all day, all day dormant—
a small winter in here

amidst the clutch of January,
its arm I can't see
yet sense, the whole shinning hose
and spiraling-wire business
taped to a duct in the joists above,
all bent at the elbows
in unkind contortions, some

forced configuration for the vent,
for the event of my head,
its hollow thought,
as if a mien might occupy
the space of its ghost:
Dead, I would have never held,
never had a rutabaga.

Rubble

Sunset in the city.
One sees the herd
of heavy equipment's quit:
black crane among
a dozen yellow dozers,
shepherd and sheep spent,
the chain-links clinks
of tread gone quiet,
as if oiled, finally,
by its own silence.

No apocalypse, this—
just dust and random drops,
a rash of rain enough
to glaze asphalt and
toppled concrete blocks,
though in no rush,
as the sheen collects,
connects all dots,
as if to mask the sham,
the shame, of eminent domain.

Dream: The Piano Thief

You hear it bounce—
Beethoven's Fifth:
down-down-down-Dawn—
& know he's on
one end at the
bottom of the stairs
on the landing,

the piano
thief, & the only logical
reason you seem
to be so blind
is that he cleverly
closed the keys
so that neither

by moon nor star
light were you able
to perceive—let
alone conceive
of—a crime so
brazenly cold
as the coal black

of pianos
themselves, the true,
the actual
victims in this
rash of awful
burglaries
that must cease.

The Telling

It was a day like every other,
his silence telling the story begun,

"It is a day like any other," that
what had come

had gone and,
as to "another," there was none.

Still, it was impossible to tell
from him (whom she loved

without a qualm)
he feigned the truth—

not in what he told
or didn't tell,

but in the telling itself.
The telling. The telling

took on a life of its own.
The telling told on itself.

Of Angels and Aviaries

The Chamber

I believe I'll treat myself to the elevator
tonight instead of stairs. When there's no one
here sometimes I like to splurge. I figure
the place owes me a few kilowatts as it is.

Once aboard I often think it my decompression
chamber. My sinuses seem to float, there's a bird
with a funny little chirp that lets me know
exactly where I am when I count, and a kindly

angel to offer me a nudge when it's time to get
off. Fortunately, in this chamber there isn't any
music, for I would be reminded of some of my
worst intervals, the cumulative hours spent on

hold, trying to avoid the sour faces of great
composers in limbo. No, I can think of no hymn,
no dirge that would be appropriate as I am slowly
lowered upright by ropes or, more precisely, some

elaborate system of pulleys and cables, machine
I've never laid eyes on nor seen a picture of,
let alone understood the nature of gravity
of being always at the ready, even in the dark hours.

Iron Noir Reverie

Unsought, unseen,
a big old crow's beak,
piano-key black, surge of
its squawk caught, sharp yet flat
behind predawn's curtain,
tail peppered with salt
of ricocheting sleet.

A Murder in Broad Daylight

How they seem
Seen from beneath
Bats gone acrobats

Or foreign swarm
A mid-century reel
Of aerial world war

Revolving about
An undulating core
Paths erratic as

A monster moth's
Though black which
Stiches sky blue

Till one in satin cloth
Less daft deftly
Lights on a lamp's

Arching overhang
While others laugh
Their sore craws off

Gulls

From a hole in the heavens
they seem to come
one by one, low, though
formless this clock-wise flock.

It is as if by lot
a chosen speaks for them,
their silence as angry as him
of whom you'd swear

there is reason in—
though not to warn—his call,
intermittent, anonymous
as the wail of the lost.

Yet it is not sound
nor emotion
that has you stare
so long

and beyond into an ocean
of sky but the way
they seem to tread
the wind, O Lord of the amphibian

and God of gulls
to whom you pray
with faith now in the finite
with angels coming to life.

Allies

The living
lurking
but one rung
down
the ladder,
why deny
loss up top
stalks, too,
the rock dove
circling
our backyard
clearing

(flutter
and stop,
flutter
and stop,
its rush
of wings
on hinges
of rust
haunt
like an oil-
starved wheel
on carts of
the homeless)

as if trapped
in an aviary

over the spot,
an oval
of feathers
the ashes
of its mate,
grackles
still
squawking,
flocking,
hastening
away,
for a while—
carcass
in its clutches—
the hawk.

Limb

To pass this deciduous stand in wind
is to hear there is an invisible
door crows, flocking, flap through—once raucous and
now quiet, as though Ahab's leg, the flesh
stripped, bone gone gray, hangs on its creaking hinge.

Skywalk

Nights you pass
beneath
just right light
that's cast
on the black
asphalt
a mirror
appears
to mirror
the stars
when then it
swiftly
disappears,
reverts
to a thing
real as
pea gravel
rolled flat
as if to
sheerest
clear crystals
of quartz,
rock candy
without
quintessence
without
dimension
without,
thus, number.

Telepathy

With reason then to be believed in when,
unschooled in solitude as he could be,
he held the receiver to dial his girl,
stopped, and with a silence flooding the house,
its furnace turning mute, with all outside
an April snowfall inexplicably
opaque, transmogrifying phone to bone
gone black within his grasp, there was science,
its disquieting air, with which it seemed
at himself he stared, a person unknown
though sensed there, manifest in the abstract—
that subtle rosette, its cluster of holes,
those perfect petals absent a dial tone,
then—without even a hint of a ring—
a refrain, the thinnest name, maybe his,
that came with her faint question, "Are you there?"

Tennis Without a Net

This was a dish with legs,
great legs, speed skater legs
fit for tights in super hero comics

and more bare than tan on the court.
What, if not incombustible lust,
sparked a lifetime of voyeuristic sport

as she paired off with the spoon—
a tall kid she called Frank, known to us
as a hot dog if ever there was one—

a phallic gesture from her if ever I saw one,
though I knew not what but the finger to call it then,
blind to big words like *psychology*, deaf to *Freud*.

Yet hardly void of self-consciousness. Full of it,
in fact, so that it didn't hit
me how the cow doesn't come home in the myth,

O moonshot for the divine by the bovine,
O caterwaul of the fiddle for the feline,
O spontaneous combustion too inert for her to diddle with.

The Drama King Walks It Off

Ah, this autumnal itch, the switch—August
cacophony gone to cacophonies,
you troop of minute Thespians under
foot, acrobats with the breeze at your backs.

Unlike Olivier's blond, black-roots prince,
I own no admonition, though the click-
clacking cartwheels that are your herd has me
in, if not the scene, that game frame of mind.

I shall not follow you to asphalt's end
but pivot home where, brooding, I began,
whilst perhaps yon Bloodhound pup adorning
the approaching pickup, snout thrust clear out
in its olfactory rush, jowls howling,
senses scent of escape from our burning.

Camping at Hartman Creek

(for “a table for twenty-seven”)

Chores over, struck
by a quick chorus of uproarious voices
like axes echoing off oak,
he remembers back toward Wapaca,

the corner of County Highways Q and QQ,
how sometimes language must be mute
in order to be exact
instead of accidentally cute.

Glistening now in dappled shade,
for once he’s free to cease to hear,
sees his way clear to seize the obvious:

a wine cooler whistling in the wind . . .
a farmer’s match flicked
careening mid-air
like a grasshopper sprung from the thicket.

He’s quiet for the moment
and for the moment cautious,
far from house yet near to home
as the site itself.

What if he had known?
That to remain here might mean
the promise of a life’s work.

Hunch

I put my right sock on inside out. Always.
—Dan Majerle

1.
Is it so different for the guy who
puts both socks on right side out every time?
What if the right turns out to be the left?
You never know when you might be in an
accident, as if the emergency
room nurse would not know before you arrived
you were a fool or that her clairvoyance
was not rooted in self-knowledge. Let's say
for argument's sake she is the Angel
of Mercy and as such not a gambler.
Would she not have on gloves? Would you know her
breasts as ballast for invisible wings?
Now *there* are unanswerable questions.
But as to why our good angel might look—
always—at one card at a time every
hand she is dealt is not a mystery.
She must distinguish the heart from the spade
let alone deduce the ace from the deuce.
There are livings to be made. Dan Majerle's
trainer was trying to heal a blister.
Whether God spoke to him through a textbook
or thunder, whether he hangs a rabbit's
foot on his belt, keeps a penny in his
sneaker—all that matters is his horseshoe
does not dent the hardwood, that the friction

is somehow reduced whether the method
be matter of fact, the stuff of fiction,
or child of their union, intuition.

2.
I, myself, confess to a litany
of superstitions. For the better part
of my life I prayed. Now I write poems.
You are reading one of them, which, before
I began, I hoisted salt over my
left shoulder, "yellow pellets" they call it
at the Piggly Wiggly, for our water
softener, a forty pound bag of it
that, before I picked up a pen, had me
counting old maids in a popcorn bowl.
One hundred-forty-three. I was off by
a sizable margin—fifty-three to
be exact (or fifty-two, depending
upon whether we should count the one that
got away, squirting as it did between
my forefinger and thumb)—yes, a goodly
number more than what I guessed it would be.
See, I have this thing. If I tell myself
"no *way*" something is about to happen,
I'm betting on my hunch it will happen.
It's like leaving your basketball behind
on your way to a Bucks game and heading
around the corner of the stadium
and there stands, poised to sign it, Abe Lincoln.
Well, Dan Majerle ain't Abraham Lincoln.
On the other hand, Abe will never shoot
a three. Yet neither did Dave Cowens, whose

autograph I suddenly saw there through
my drool on the display case in, of all
places, Sheboygan, the one signature
I'd always wanted and known I'd never
own, the very one that for five dollars
I do own, ink that made me think he who
doesn't seek also finds, superstitious
I'm more often not, confident I'll not
possess so much as the dot in the "i"
of *Lincoln*, though the "j" in *Majerle*—swish—
is entirely a different story.

From the Bottom of a Jar of Honey

Fine as incandescent filament,
Thin as the lowest-test nylon fishing line,
As a fly-away strand of corn silk in sudden sunlight
Or the summoned, slick sensation of lanugo on a new-born,
Still it stretches from the hand, which hovers over crust of cornbread,
Vertical as a magician's charmed rope, yet coiling at bottom to
    quickly melt,
Unwound, finally, off a silver spoon, as if from a golden spool—
    this archangel's drool.

Brush Strokes

(from *Nimrod* "doing the one hundreds")

One honey of a dreaded count's one shy:
ninety-nine when, Dude, you're the lone shepherd
even a Stetson from Sheplers don't hide.

Heck, what with her digital glowing 1:00
under your silver dollar sun, it's time
now you pen yourself in, 10 x 10—Lord
damn that lost heifer, the whole herd, before
red becomes you and you become rawhide—
escape to her room, your phantom cowgirl
doing her hair, whom you pine with rime for.

A Prose Poem

A prose poem
I do not remember the name of
nor who wrote it
so deep is it down
the swift river
I have waded against thus far

has a man
looking into the back
of an old-time radio

And what he sees
is not the gleaming tubes
the dark columns
nor the silver pillboxes

but their aggregate
a miniature metropolis

Being of the mind
that makes its own movies
I too had seen that cityscape
and have longed to live
in a realm without windows

a town in the abstract
pristine as it would be
without detail keen enough

to perceive the vehicles
let alone little people

I suppose it is the eye of the hermit
in want of the eye of God
which leads one to value
for a time
great loneliness

I know it is what drives me on country roads
(when I should have taken the highway)
to apprehend without warning
(as might the man in the prose poem)
hurling over a horizon

a knee-high city
in the form of a country graveyard

Stone

You do not clamor
for the weight of your.

It's the aura of
you have come to love.

It's the fervent squeeze
of eyelids that frees.

There are there blank words,
no angels, no birds.

Triads

Achromatics

These words like counter
glass you see yet don't perceive,
should pearls be beneath:

Although the prism's
prison, how it appears to
be whole to the mole.

*

Passion's flag unfurled.
Whole nations brought to their knees.
Color with a past.

*

Poets love the myth
it has no rhyme, sweet sister
to lemon and lime.

*

From a child's drawing
the light of utopia:
school bus with a flat.

*

Little men from Mars
camouflaged by dark and stars,
choking on cigars.

*

Dead TV, cold couch,
dust on the floor–elephant
we couldn't ignore.

*

Hue of such huge range,
shades even heaven's not seen:
sea, sky, moon, nor men.

*

Heart? Or hero's art:
life to him is just luck to
the people eater.

*

This pigment got too
much sun, this sow in her house,
its tongue out its mouth.

*

It may be awful
small. Room for a bed. Haunted.
But O the woodwork!

Miniatures

Nude

Crude or divine—our
nature's true face in the flesh,
past, present, future.

History

Portal to the past,
the artist's eye is its own
anachronism.

Self Portrait

There you are and here
I am. The likeness is all.
Behind is no wall.

Panel

Pearl in a setting
of pearls. Pearl's lone syllable
becomes thus plural.

Mural

If not the body
through walls, at least the mind through
reality's plane.

Landscape

Outdoors indoors. Sound
turned down with the window closed
for sake of escape.

Still Life

Gone to seed, gone to
bone, this fruit whose best suit still
hangs in the closet.

Figure with Skull

Knock knock. Who's there? *Heir.*
Heir who? *Heir to your fortune.*
Take a deep breath, son.

Madonna and Child

How merry's Mary,
how married, when the old man's
not in the picture.

Man of Sorrows

Trinity's torture:
thorn, nail, sword. We get the point,
poor bleeding bastards.

Study in Red

O murder most foul,
wheelbarrow of rust beside
the stained chopping block.

Charcoal

Black sans ash—contrast,
caviar for the palate
of purest purist.

Mosaic

The atoms hold high
their placards at the far end
of the stadium.

L'Hommage

Rodin: *The Thinker*

Originally
called *The Poet*. What on Earth
was Rodin thinking?

Rodin: *Mignon*

He who says beauty's
in the eye has not held her
body in the dark.

Rodin: *The Kiss*

His is not the touch
of the master, hand on her
hip, shadow of thumb.

Rodin: *The Kiss* (II)

Her arm flung around
him hard, she's up on her toes
to lie upon him.

Rodin: *Fugit Amor*

Lovers back-to-back,
trapped, with mouths that say agape,
"Hell's a wall of air."

Rodin: *The Thinker* (II)

So absorbed, his right
shoulder and hand tucked inward—
sweet intuition.

Rodin: *Hanako*

The actress dons her
own mask—holes for the irises
she can't hide behind.

Rodin: *The Man with the Broken Nose*

Someone's right thumb left
a dent in this shiny black
aluminum man.

Rodin: *The Age of Bronze*

Clutch a tuft of hair
on top of your head. With your
free hand, cock a spear.

Rodin: *Balzac*

Balls he had as did
Rodin: genius in the guise
of a proud penis.

Rodin: *The Thinker* (III)

All life leads to this:
a bent back, elbow, and wrist—
a chin on a fist.

Three Sisters—A Study in June Sunlight

How is it that they sit, having sat,
situated in such a way that
sitting for their portraiture

insists itself upon us? What voyeurs
are we to have traveled thus, us here,
the church of art, to worship within

a certain slant seized outside, in that
Tarbell put down in paint what ain't
as much American as much as cast

in the fashion of the French, absent fusion.
Art tells a story or won't, we're taught.
Here it does and does not. Back then,

children were seen but unmentioned,
yet here's a' *int* of fondness for an infant
in the lap of—likely—its mother

(mom's smile downcast, as is her visage,
while her sisters' faces seem rendered
so as to amplify presence of an other).

Ladies—nary of the night—unite. Why
the static chat, its atmosphere farthest from
foremost adored, for most among the male

of your species is less vested in overt acts
of assignation. Oh, you can paint yourselves up
in flames that would have you fain, but what,

what a boy from Unincorporated, Wisconsin—or
Boston, even—wants you to objectify
in the end is, alas, not ass but a lass with class

sans this astigmatism, that fuzzy quality a.k.a.
Impressionism, plein air, whatever . . . yes, there
are those whose prescription, whose horn-rimmed

glasses, reveal subjects more corporeal,
albeit immortal for the moment
in a sprint against the changing light, meaning

against time, for the artist knows what
a man wants in a woman is what a woman
wants more—herself perpetually in her

prime, at once as fertile and as pure as
starlight into daylight, dawn, then dappled
light, like moonlight by noon light,

like the ideal superimposed upon the real,
wheel shy spindle, or, in another century,
shown thrown on screen, the frames in the reel.

Ars Poetica

The Canon

You know the protocol
as the flag first and then the flagbearer
appear over the rise in your psyche.

That oligarchy of one
in the form of an Uncle Sam,
his top hat in hand, he's come to collect.

You've tried hiding in the city of Abandon
but there he was again, that hat on
on every billboard and poster,

that right, erect index finger
over his pursed lips, whispering,
"Shhhhhh"

It's a shame he's never learned his place,
his status as shadow of the past
and not a form that blocks the sun.

You sing what you see can't be sung.
Luckily for you you know the tune.
You become the instrument of silence.

You think, what is the sense of this,
the meaning of meaning, if only to keep his secrets.
You write you ought to rather have had Tourette's.

Writer's Block

There is no such thing . . . .
—Philip Dacey

Just as this starkest,
dark interior
appears as vivid
as a veiled mirror,
so seems reflection's
ear for unsung song,
wound chiasmic sound—
silence thus unbound.

Ars Poetica

See here, poets, why seem so insistent
on ink darkening the dawn, on donning
ego with widespread wing, if not hell bent
on seizing from silence the will to sing?

You'll not know which is, youngbards sans bitches,
the impetus, until you remember
the cave, the chains, the wall, how he switches—
your archrival—to anger from amber,

the shock, its sock (raw tease?) that sucks, as does
his Republic, its hum-drum hymn he hums
that real is less than ideal (O because
Flesh is but shadow of the soul!) and thumbs

his nose at those poor bastards—cave's conscripts—
among them, you can bet, the banned poets,
malcontents, miscreants whose manuscripts
enrich through the spirit of no regrets.

So be not a slave to the source of scorn.
As maker your soul's made and is not born.

The Dead Give-Away

If they want you to put trust in Jesus,
they ought not hoodwink you into Santa
Claus, a dead give-away being Timex—
not the Captain Midnight watch you watched tick
uptown at the store, your scribbled wish-for
listing beneath a drawer Clark Kent alone
with x-ray vision could decipher, with
bigger glasses, in all that blue pizazz
on Mom's wreathed tablet sheet you stole away.
Quiet as the snuffed wick in its smoking
jar of wax, you asked, headed to bed, if
maybe like his elf you blew it out, he'd
visit, cuz catch a glimpse and he won't stop.

Winning the Future

That mod-looking hussy and her Honda
Odyssey—well ain't she swell, sweet, struttin'
up the street in gold bangles and red sweats,
keys in hand, taillights flashing, bleating beep.
Mad as a badger with lead poisoning,
it's P.M.S. from M.P.S. Cork your
questions, kids. Go a.) red b.) reed c.) read
X-Box. Bargaining is her a.) rite b.)
write c.) right (albeit not natural).
Freedom's dumb, something to shun, won't rime with
coercion, the union variety,
voluntary sans "in" and all that jazz—
jus, her right, someone else's sacrifice.

The Poet Addresses His Complex

Hark, Old Hydra-head, which one among you
cautions I'm plumb nuts? So what I sound angry?
It's a congenital condition, this,
my murmur, its finite number amidst
all of your mumbling mumbo jumbo.
Desire desires, I say—a Valentine
gone unread. Not like our friend Stanford, Frank,
who stuck a three-tined fork in his ticker—
never mind head, temple (its potential
quicker)—as if in a done, rare rolled rump,
zinging his own strings, strumming with a thumb
fingering the trigger. So kiss my ax,
Jacks. I'm rhythm, rhyme, and your leitmotiv.

The Poem That Writes Itself

Its blood is black and the same can be said
of the rest of its features, creatures that
crawl like schooled and disciplined ranks of ants
to—quiet trope—quick as a clot, halt.

Still, the poem that writes itself is read
in redress, though we are deaf to the drat
and dread of poets' dead-silent moments,
internal infernal bleating, mime's vault

of time's inert volcanos that then hide
their ashes, those erasures which were once
sparks, till the poem that *won't* write itself

seems borne of its own accord to abide
beside heaven's brethren, without an ounce
of onus as dust thrust upon the shelf.

E Pluribus Unum Poem

The have-nots and haves of the Virginias—
can you hear them in fractured Michigan,
though less so in Orlando, Florida,
(Boise of an inverted Idaho)
among tourists diverse as Hawaii
in maybe Anaheim, California?

O, say it ain't so in the Dakotas,
kinda contained kinda like Rhode Island
(no more an island than Indiana)—
desolate like eastern Colorado
and weathered as a shack in Kentucky
flat as a dock in Louisiana.

Or how right and wrong the Carolinas,
Charleston a mink worn in Wyoming
on one for whom home is Oklahoma
(that pan in the hand of New Mexico
in place of pot). Pious Mississippi,
her once insipid sis Alabama—

are they free? Is there access to Texas?
I remember Ft. Lewis, Washington—
conscripted, then flown via Alaska
to occupied Naha where *Ohayo*
was all I'd decipher. A Tennessee
volunteer whose bride hailed from Nebraska

got shipped back, in stir, near her in Kansas.
Here's hope grunts don't elope in Maryland
nor go AWOL with WACS from Iowa—
lesbians they were with an Arkansas
first sergeant and a covert New Jersey
horse connection through Ft. Gordon, Georgia,

bragged about too often. Massachusetts
was what we all called their lawyer, a Maine
man, "main line" meaning train to Montana
to him. May the law be a beaut in Utah,
too, though, be it blue, undone—New Hampshire,
where to warn presidents turned Nevada

whores *We won't have it in Connecticut*!
So what's the state of sin in Wisconsin?
Any quota yet in Minnesota?
Let talk be not like syrup from Vermont,
the object of thought "What did Delaware,
if anything?" Should Pennsylvania

prove to be paved, burb and lot of New York,
you owe me a postcard, Dour Oregon,
sent somewhere hot though not Arizona.
Swear, live by this: no noise in Illinois
till you cross the bridge into Missouri
where misery won't rime with Missoura.

Magic Act

Do not fool yourself.
You do not believe in magic.

You believe in mystery.
You're here because

I am art, masked as if
in the velvet voice of

the magician, which
shall have appeared

in time to disappear
into the tall, black

folds of memory.
Should mere wonder

turn lust for illusion,
you mustn't close your eyes

to closing your eyes
in presence of this absence

that shall materialize.

www.ingramcontent.com/pod-product-compliance
Ingram Content Group UK Ltd.
Pitfield, Milton Keynes, MK11 3LW, UK
UKHW041315190726
13845UKWH00025B/294

9 789363 548770